STEP INTO SCIENCE

THE BODY

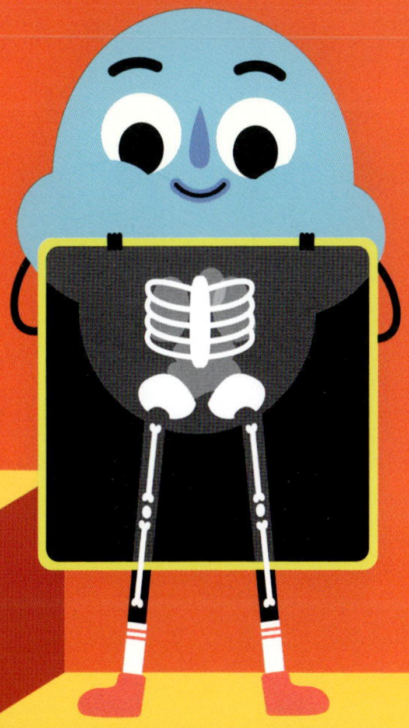

PETER RILEY

Enslow PUBLISHING

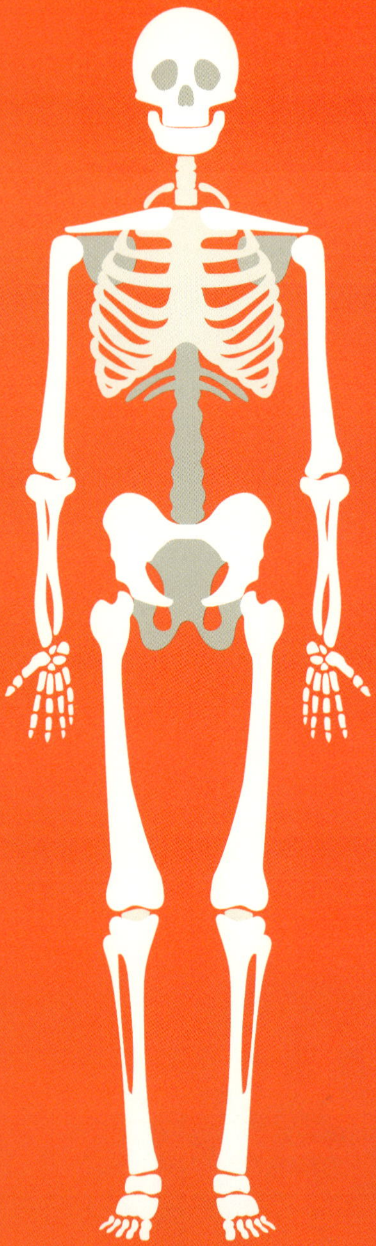

Published in 2025 by Enslow Publishing, LLC
2544 Clinton Street
Buffalo, NY 14224

First published in Great Britain in 2023 by Hodder & Stoughton

The text in this book was previously published in the series *Moving Up with Science*.

To my granddaughter, Holly Jane.

Editor: Elise Short
Design and Illustration: Collaborate Ltd

Manufactured in the United States of America

CPSIA compliance information: Batch #CW25ENS: For further information contact Enslow Publishing LLC, New York, New York at 1-800-398-2504.

Please visit our website, www.enslowpublishing.com. For a free color catalog of all our high-quality books, call toll free 1-800-398-2504 or fax 1-877-980-4454.

Cataloging-in-Publication Data

Names: Riley, Peter.
Title: The body / Peter Riley.
Description: Buffalo, NY : Enslow Publishing, 2025. | Series: Step into science | Includes glossary.
Identifiers: ISBN 9781978541627 (pbk.) | ISBN 9781978541634 (library bound) | ISBN 9781978541641 (ebook)
Subjects: LCSH: Human body--Juvenile literature. | Human physiology--Juvenile literature. | Human anatomy--Juvenile literature.
Classification: LCC QP37.R55 2025 | DDC 612--dc23

We recommend adult supervision at all times while doing the activities in this book. Also, please be sure to do the following before starting an activity in which they are applicable (not all safety tips will apply to all activities):

- Wear an apron and cover surfaces.
- Tie back long hair.
- Ask an adult for help with cutting.
- Check materials for allergens.

CONTENTS

Words in **bold** can be found in the glossary on pages 28–29.

ANIMAL BODIES

Animal bodies come in all sorts of shapes and sizes. Some bodies have two leg; some have four, six, eight, thirty, or more; and some have no legs at all. Bodies can be covered with skin, hair, feathers, or scales. Humans are animals with two legs and a body covered with skin and hair.

SIGNS OF LIFE

All bodies carry out seven activities of life. The first six are breathing, feeding, moving, using your **senses** to find out about your surroundings, getting rid of waste, and growing. The seventh takes place when an animal is fully grown. This is reproduction, or making new animals.

Animal bodies have different coverings. The large body of a rhinoceros is covered in tough skin. The smaller body of a bird is covered in feathers.

BODY PARTS

A body has many parts. The human body is divided into a head, **torso**, and limbs (arms and legs). Most body parts are hidden from view. They are inside the body, under the skin. Each body part or organ carries out different activities that help keep the body alive. For example, the heart pumps blood around the body, and the lungs control breathing.

In this book, we will be looking at the parts of the body that help us move and the parts that help us eat and digest our food.

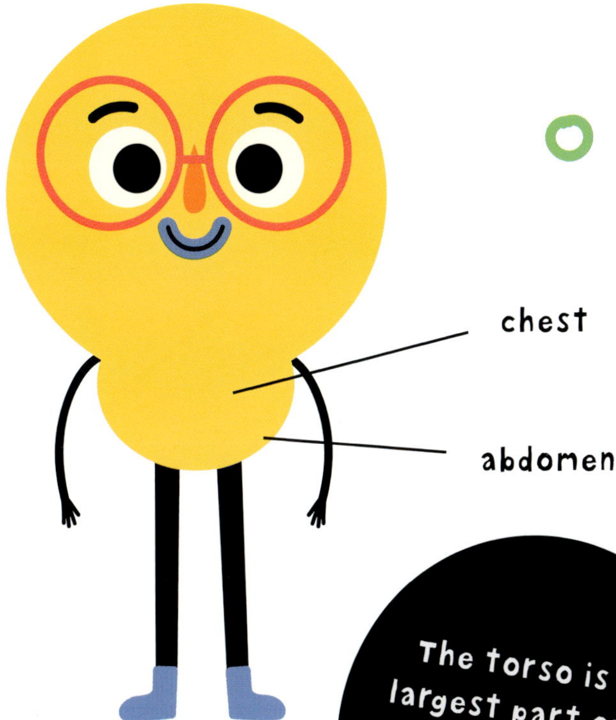

The torso is the largest part of the body. It is divided into the chest and the abdomen.

Early scientists found out what was inside a body by cutting open bodies of dead animals, such as frogs and mice.

Today, scientists can use **X-ray** machines and **MRI scanners** to see inside living bodies. This MRI scan shows the **brain** inside the human head.

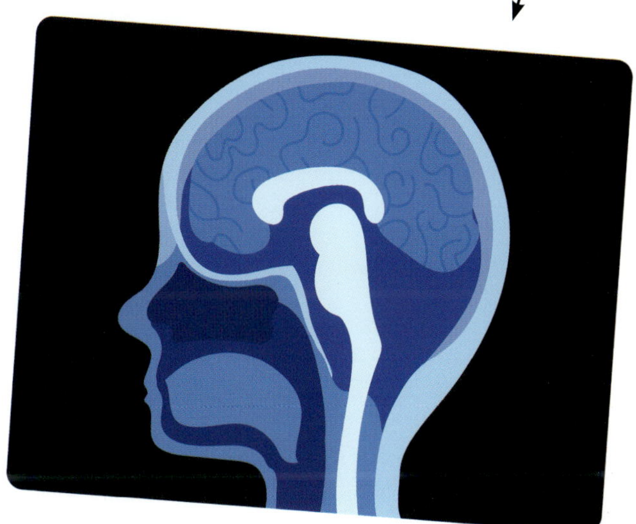

THE HUMAN SKELETON

Many animals have skeletons, including humans. The human skeleton is inside the body. It performs three tasks. It gives us support, it protects parts of our body, and it helps us move.

SUPPORT

The skeleton is made of strong, hard bones. The bones fit together to hold us up. If you did not have a skeleton you would be very floppy!

PROTECTION

The bones of the skull form a hard case to protect your brain. The bones of your ribs make a cage, which protects your heart and lungs. The backbone protects the **spinal cord**, which is made of **nerves** that connect your brain to the rest of your body.

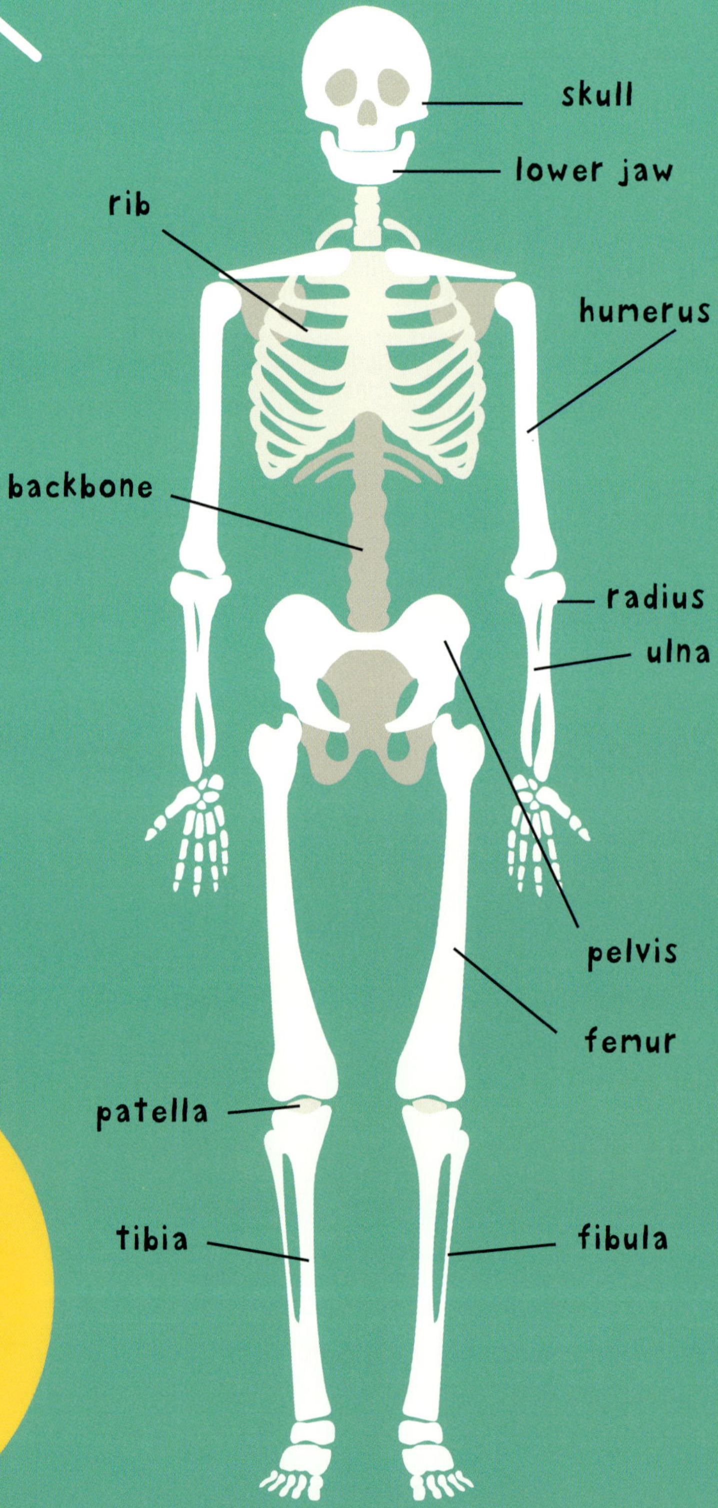

The largest bone in the human skeleton is in the leg above the knee. The smallest bones are found deep inside the ears.

MOVEMENT

The place where two bones meet is called a joint. Most joints allow bones to move. The end of each bone is covered in smooth **cartilage** to help the bones move more easily. Bones are connected to joints with tough **ligaments**, which hold them firmly in place.

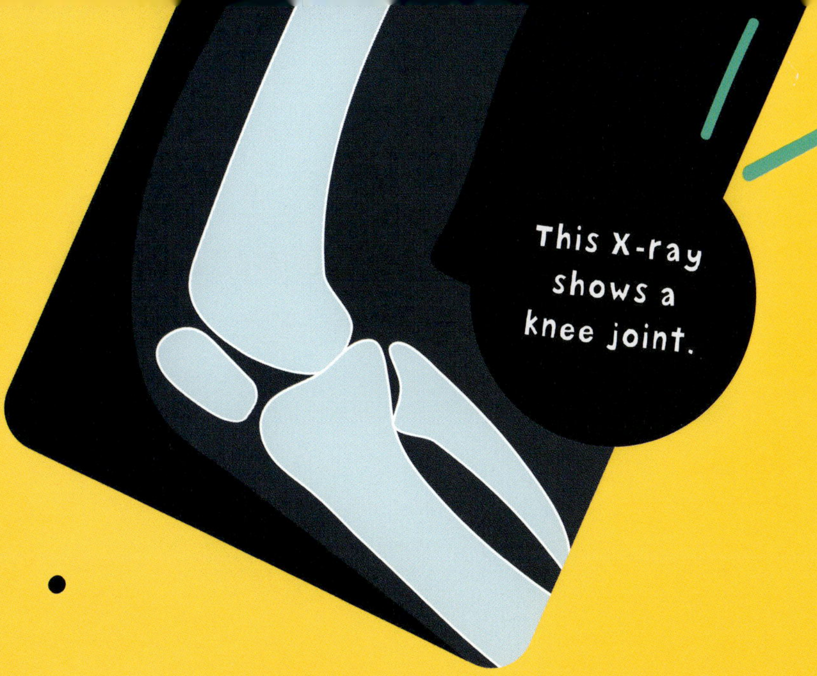

PAPER BONES

Scientists sometimes make models to use in experiments. Find out if thicker bones are stronger than thinner bones by making model bones out of rolled-up newspaper.

EQUIPMENT:

- rolls of paper in a variety of thicknesses
- water bottle

1 Hold a thin paper roll between your hands. Put an empty water bottle on it, and put a box underneath to catch it if it falls. Fill the bottle with some water, and seal it before putting it back on the paper. Repeat this until the roll bends.

2 Repeat the experiment with a thicker paper roll. The thicker the roll, the more weight it can carry before it bends. The thicker your bones, the stronger they are. Your leg bones are thick. This makes them strong enough to support your whole body.

MUSCLES

There are over 600 muscles in your body. Muscles make a body move.

HOW MUSCLES WORK

Muscles are attached to the skeleton. When a muscle **contracts**, it can make a bone or bones move. It also gets shorter and feels harder.

Each muscle moves a part of the body. Certain parts of the body, such as the arm, need several muscles to help them move.

You can feel your muscles move if you frown. Now stick your fingers in your cheeks and smile. When you smile, the muscles in your cheeks contract. Seventeen muscles are used to make you smile.

TENDONS

Muscles are attached to bones by **tendons**. You can feel them in the inside of your elbow joint when you bend your arm. You can also feel them at the back of the knee when you sit down.

WORKING TOGETHER

Once a muscle has become short and hard, it needs help to relax and lengthen. Muscles are arranged so that when one muscle moves and gets shorter, another muscle stretches, ready to pull it back. You can investigate how two muscles in your arm work together.

1 Make your right arm straight. Push the fingers of your left hand into the front muscle at the top of your arm. This muscle is called the biceps. Now, bend your arm. How does the biceps muscle feel now?

2 Now keep your arm bent and push the fingers of your left hand into the back muscle at the top of your arm. This is called the triceps muscle. Straighten your arm again. How does your triceps muscle feel as you move your arm back?

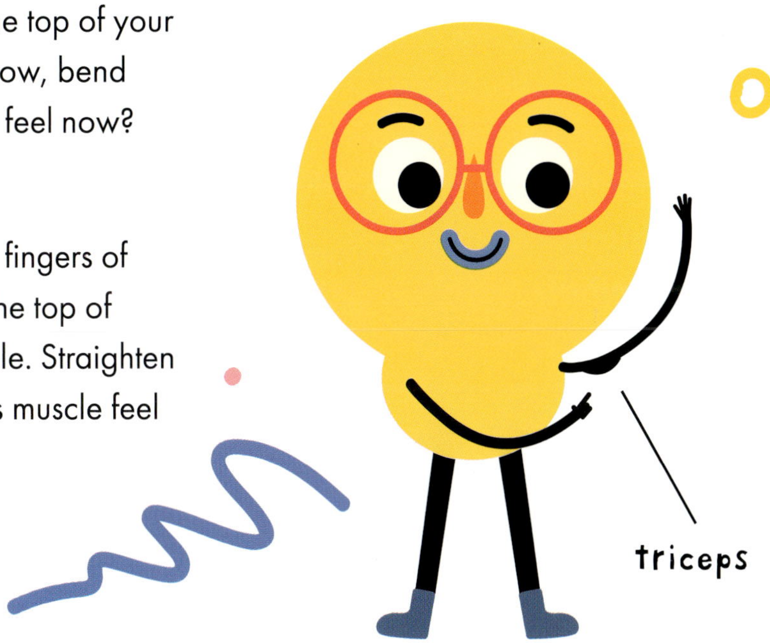

WHAT HAPPENS TO YOUR BICEPS AND TRICEPS WHEN YOU STRAIGHTEN YOUR ARM?

ANIMAL SKELETONS

Animals can be divided up into two groups according to the type of skeleton they have. Animals that have a backbone and a skeleton made of bone and cartilage are called vertebrates. Animals that do not have a backbone are called invertebrates.

VERTEBRATES

Vertebrates have a number of bones, all linked together by joints, which form the animal's backbone or spine. Each bone is called a **vertebra**, and lots of vertebra are called vertebrae. There are five groups of vertebrates: fish, **amphibians**, **reptiles**, birds, and **mammals**.

You can feel the vertebrae in your backbone if you rub your fingers down the middle of your back. Each lump you feel is the top of a vertebra.

INVERTEBRATES

The largest group of invertebrates is made up of animals that have a hard, protective case around their body called an **exoskeleton**. These animals are called arthropods.

They are divided into four sub-groups: insects; centipedes and millipedes; spiders and scorpions; and crustaceans.

A stag beetle is an insect. Its exoskeleton acts like a suit of armor to keep it safe when it fights.

WATER BODIES

Some invertebrates do not have an exoskeleton. These invertebrates include jellyfish, earthworms, and mollusks, such as snails and slugs. Some of these invertebrates, such as snails, have a shell instead.

If you watch a snail moving, you can see its muscles rippling under the shell that protects it. You can watch, but don't touch!

MOVEMENT IN ANIMALS

As in humans, muscles and skeletons work together to make vertebrates move. Each animal moves in different ways.

MOVEMENT IN FISH

The vertebrae of a fish are fixed together with lots of joints so that the backbone is flexible and can bend when the muscles on either side pull on it. This helps a fish move through the water.

Muscles pull a fish's body into a curved shape, which pushes on the water and moves the fish forward.

A lizard moves by throwing both legs on one side forward at the same time.

MOVEMENT IN REPTILES AND AMPHIBIANS

Salamanders, lizards, and crocodiles have four legs and a flexible backbone. Their muscles work with their skeletons to make their bodies into an 'S' shape, which throws their legs forwards so they can walk and run.

MOVEMENT IN BIRDS

The backbone of a bird is rigid and fixed tightly to its ribs. This makes the skeleton firm enough to support the bird's flight muscles. When the flight muscles shorten and lengthen, the wings flap up and down and push on the air, which makes the bird rise up. When the wings are tipped backward and flapped, the bird moves forwards.

MOVEMENT IN INSECTS

The middle part of an insect's body is called the **thorax**. In flying insects, the thorax is packed with muscles that move the wings.

MOVEMENT IN WORMS

Worms have a body that is divided into sections called **segments**. The muscles in each segment help the worm move along. Tiny hairs on its skin help it grip the soil as it moves.

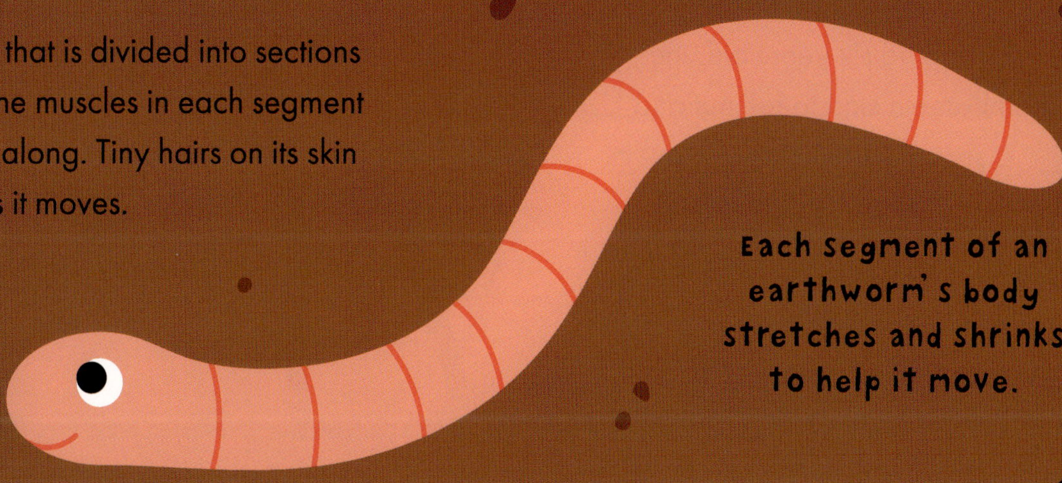

TEETH

Teeth come in different shapes and sizes according to the job they do.

Teeth are used to cut, rip, and grind food until it is small enough to swallow. Humans cut and rip food with their sharp front teeth. The tongue passes the food to big, blunt back teeth for grinding before the food is swallowed.

BABY TEETH

Humans have two sets of teeth during their lifetime: baby teeth and adult teeth. Baby teeth begin to grow through when a human is around six months old and are a complete set of 20 teeth by around three years old.

At around six years old, the milk teeth start to fall out and a second set begins to grow in their place. This adult set of 32 teeth should last for the rest of a human's life.

Teeth need to be brushed with toothpaste twice a day to make sure they stay healthy and clean.

ADULT TEETH

There are four types of adult teeth. These are incisors, canines, premolars, and molars.

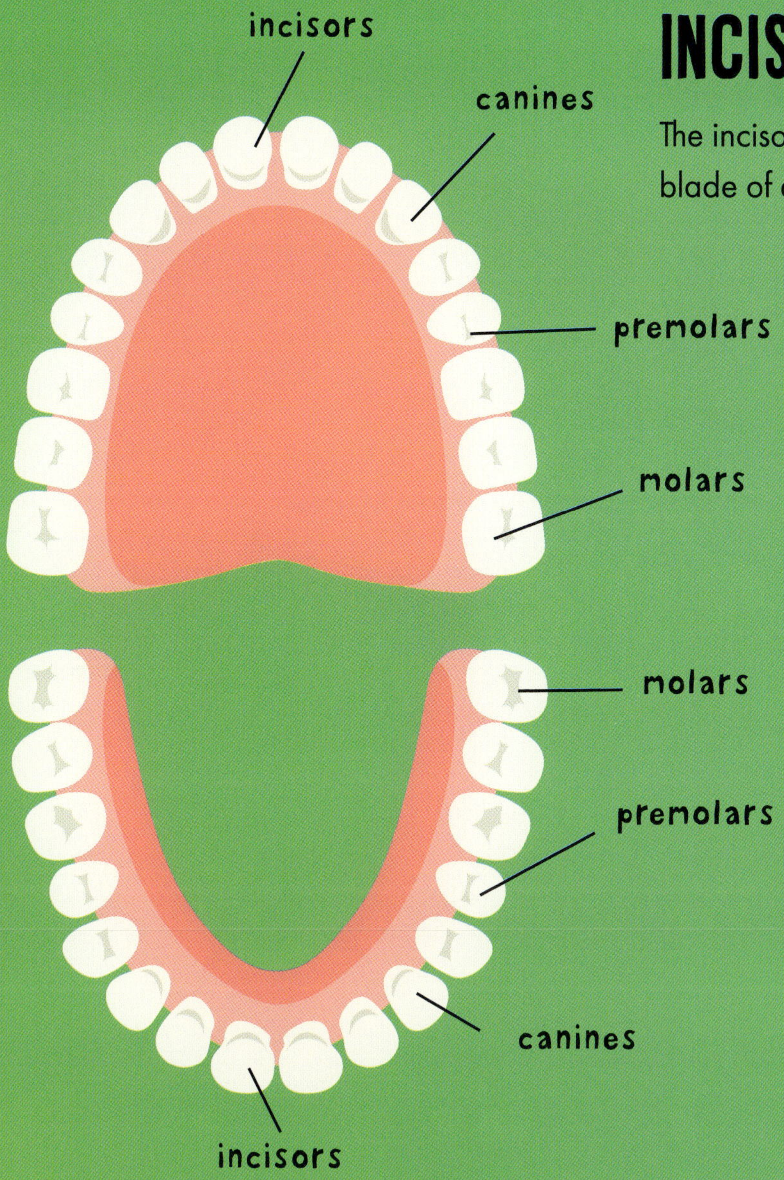

INCISORS

The incisor teeth have wide, sharp tops like the blade of a knife. We use them to bite into our food.

CANINES

The canine teeth are pointed and can look a bit like fangs. We use them to tear up tough food, such as meat.

PREMOLARS AND MOLARS

The premolars and molars have lumps called cusps, which help to grind up all types of food.

YOU CAN THINK OF THE IMAGE ABOVE AS AN ADULT TOOTH MAP. LOOK AT YOUR TEETH IN A MIRROR AND MAKE YOUR OWN TOOTH MAP. DRAW THE INCISORS, CANINES, PREMOLARS, AND MOLARS. REMEMBER, YOU MAY HAVE SOME BABY TEETH AND SOME ADULT TEETH.

THE DIGESTIVE SYSTEM

Once your teeth have made food smaller, it goes on a journey through your digestive system. Food is digested so it can pass into the blood and go to the parts of the body that need it. The digestive system uses juices to break down the food, which the body uses for energy.

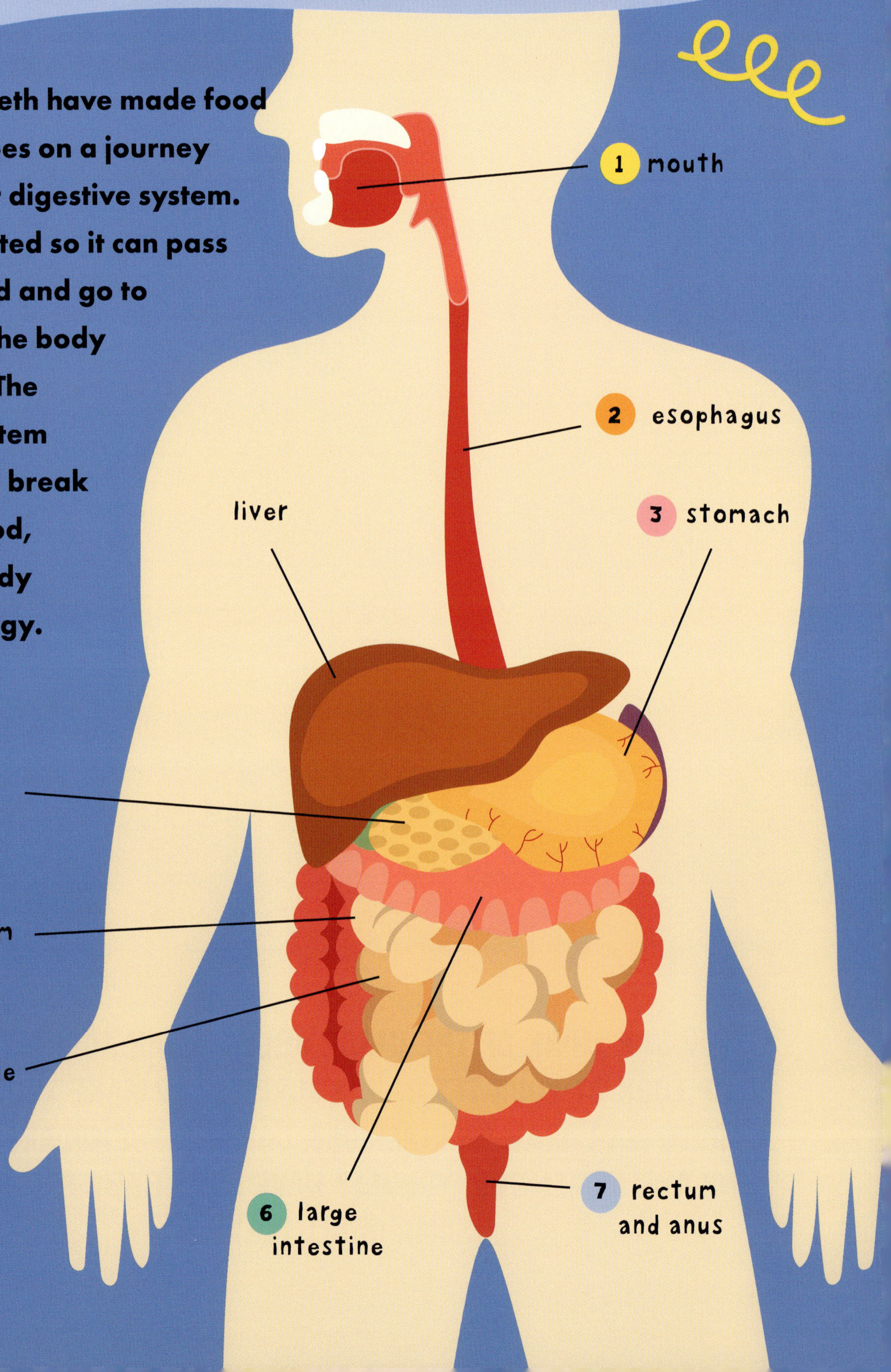

1 MOUTH

Your teeth break food into small pieces. Saliva is a **digestive juice** from your salivary **glands**, which makes your food slippery and even easier to swallow. Your tongue shapes your food into pellets, ready to pass down your esophagus.

2 ESOPHAGUS

The esophagus is a tube in your throat. Food passes down the esophagus from the back of your mouth to your stomach.

3 STOMACH

The stomach churns up food and mixes it with digestive juices. Acid in the stomach helps kill **germs** in food.

4 DUODENUM

Bile from the liver and digestive juices from the pancreas are mixed with food here.

5 SMALL INTESTINE

The small intestine makes more digestive juices to break down food further. The food then dissolves in the water that surrounds it. The wall of the small intestine **absorbs** all the **nutrients**, and they pass into the blood. The dissolved nutrients in the blood are pumped around the body by the heart. Different body parts absorb them and use them to keep the body alive.

6 LARGE INTESTINE

Undigested food passes through here and has water taken from it to be used by all parts of the body.

7 RECTUM AND ANUS

Undigested food is stored in the rectum. The waste is later released out of the body through the anus.

THE CIRCULATORY SYSTEM

The digestive system breaks down food so nutrients can be sent to all parts of the body. The system that moves nutrients around the body is the circulatory system.

THE HEART

Nearly all animals have a circulatory system powered by a heart. The heart pumps blood through the circulatory system. The circulatory system is made up of tubes that carry blood around the body.

An earthworm has tubes that act like hearts. Muscles in these tubes squeeze blood through the earthworm's circulatory system.

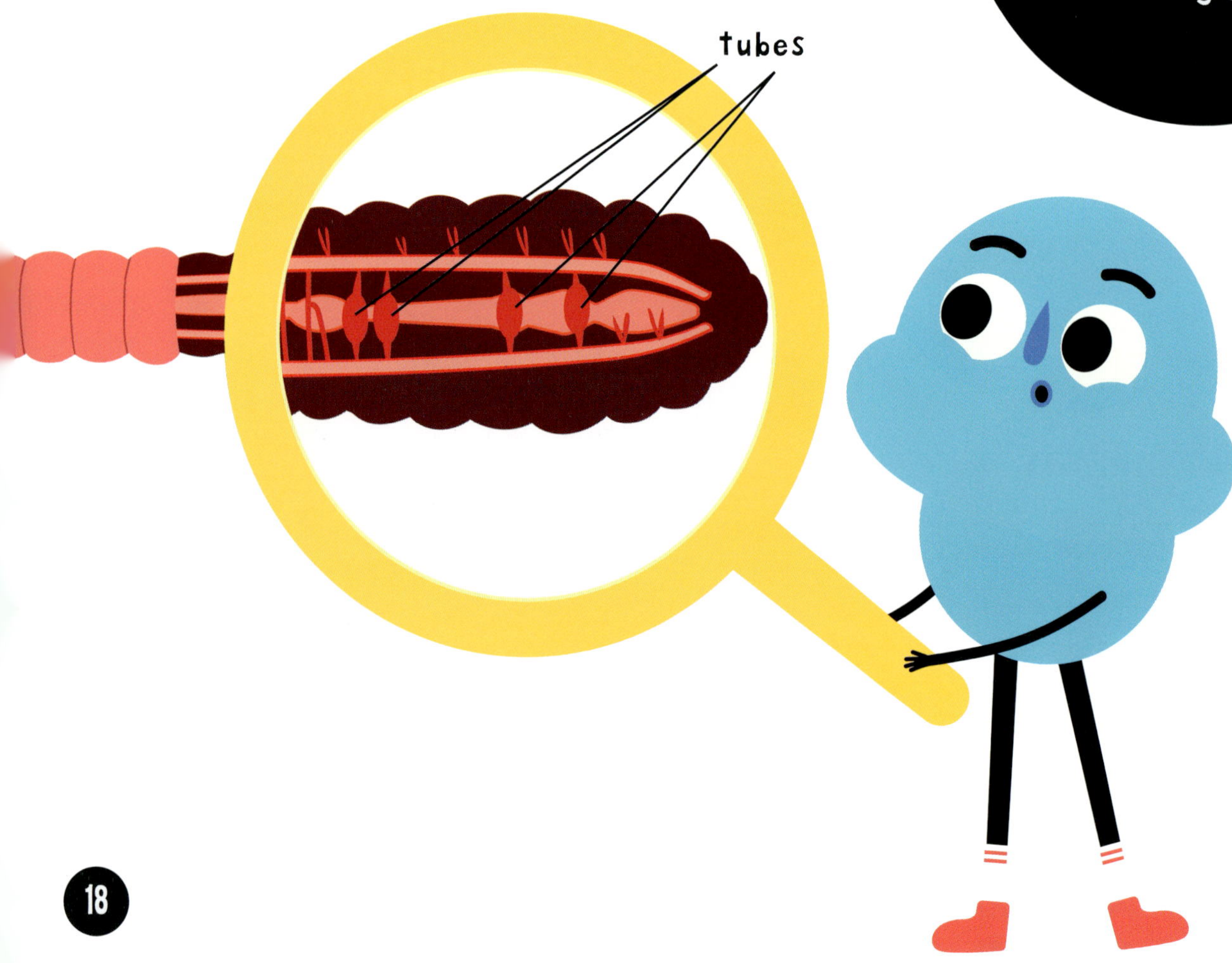

THE HUMAN CIRCULATORY SYSTEM

The heart in humans and other vertebrates is divided into sections called chambers, which collect blood from one part of the circulatory system and push it into the next part. The human heart has four chambers. The two chambers on the right side collect blood from all round the body and send it to the lungs to get **oxygen**. The two on the left side collect blood containing oxygen from the lungs and send it all round the body. Oxygen is needed by all parts of the body to help change digested food into energy.

The blue tubes taking blood to the heart are called **veins**. The red tubes taking blood away from the heart are called **arteries**.

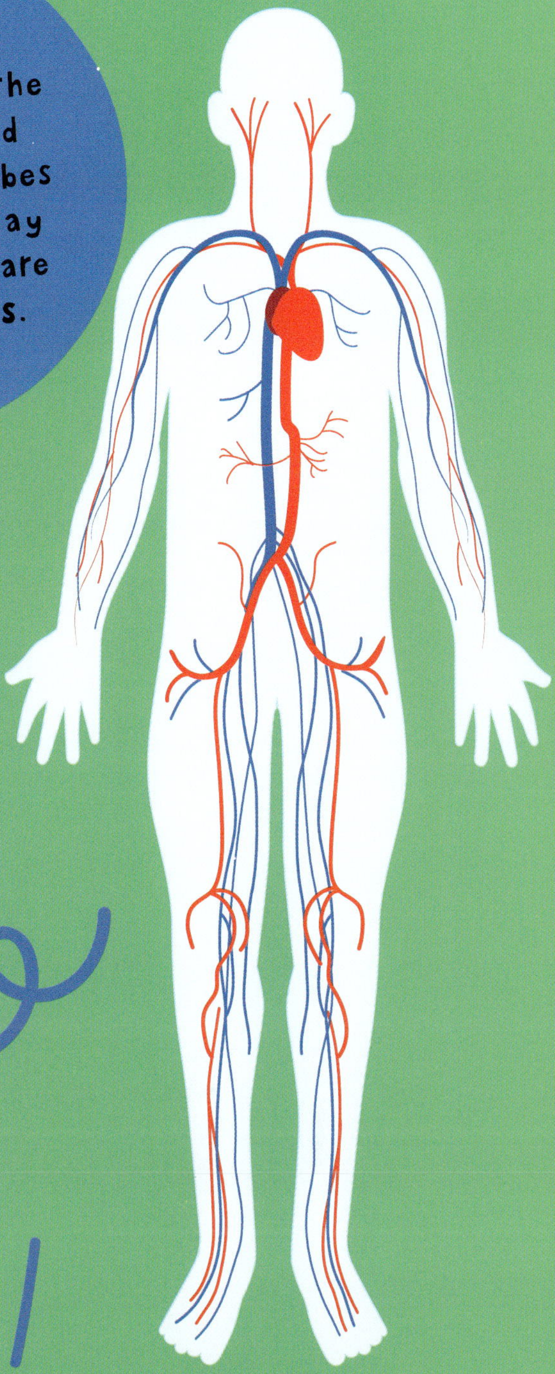

Each of the two upper chambers is called an atrium. The lower chambers are called ventricles.

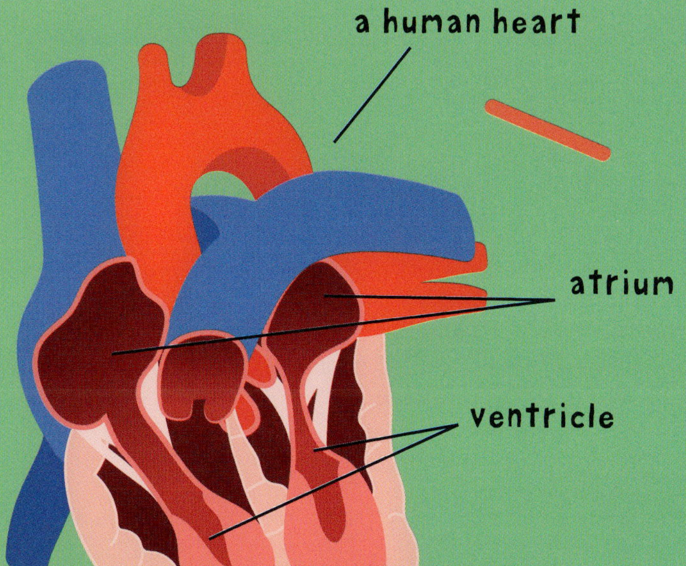

MOVING DIGESTED FOOD

All the nutrients from digested food are absorbed into the blood from the small intestine. Veins take nutrient-filled blood to the heart. The heart then pumps this blood all over the body.

NUTRIENTS

Bodies need nutrients, fiber, and water to stay alive. There are five groups of nutrients. These are proteins, fats, carbohydrates, vitamins, and minerals. Foods and drinks provide us with nutrients, fiber, and water.

Foods rich in proteins are meat, fish, beans, nuts and eggs.

PROTEINS

Proteins are needed for growth and to repair injuries to the body. They are also needed to make the juices that digest food.

Foods rich in carbohydrates include pasta, rice, and bread.

CARBOHYDRATES

Carbohydrates contain energy. As soon as a carbohydrate-rich food has been digested, the body uses the energy to keep itself alive.

VITAMINS

Vitamins help to keep the body healthy. For example, vitamin C is needed to keep blood vessels healthy and vitamin D is needed for healthy bones.

FATS

The body stores fat under the skin to keep it warm. Fat also contains energy. If the energy from carbohydrates has been used up and the body needs extra energy, it uses the energy in fats.

MINERALS

Minerals are used to build body parts, such as bones and blood.

A BALANCED DIET

Your diet is the food that you usually eat. Your body needs a certain amount of each nutrient to keep it healthy. Too much or too little of a nutrient can cause problems in the body.

A meal of pasta, meat, vegetables, and plenty of water provides many nutrients.

FOOD GROUPS

Foods are divided into groups based on the nutrients they provide. The yellow section of the picture below shows foods rich in carbohydrates. The green section shows fruits and vegetables. The blue section shows dairy products rich in calcium, which is a mineral needed for strong bones. The pink section provides protein. Treats like those in the purple section can also be part of a balanced diet.

MORE THAN JUST FUEL

Food is often seen as fuel for the body. However, it can also be much more than that. Food can provide joy, comfort, and a connection to our family history. It's important to eat foods with many different nutrients, but it's also OK to eat some foods just because they make you happy. Food can be fuel, and it can be fun!

Sweets and other treats may be delicious, but they do not contain the variety of nutrients needed to keep your body healthy and active. It's OK to eat them sometimes, but make sure to eat more nutritious foods too.

WITH HELP AND PERMISSION FROM AN ADULT, CUT OUT PICTURES OF FRESH FRUIT AND VEGETABLES FROM MAGAZINES TO CREATE A FOOD RAINBOW. TRY TO USE AS MANY DIFFERENT FRUITS AND VEGGIES AS POSSIBLE. EATING A VARIETY OF FOOD WILL GIVE YOUR BODY ALL THE NUTRIENTS IT NEEDS!

WHAT ANIMALS EAT

Animals can be divided into three groups based on what they eat: herbivores, carnivores, and omnivores.

HERBIVORES

Herbivores feed only on plants. Slugs and snails feed on leaves and are examples of invertebrate herbivores. Vertebrate herbivores include some birds, which feed on seeds, and some mammals, such as sheep and deer, which feed on grass.

The caterpillars that become moths and butterflies eat leaves. They are invertebrate herbivores.

Tortoises eat the leaves of plants. They are vertebrate herbivores.

CARNIVORES

Carnivores feed only on other animals. Invertebrate carnivores include spiders, which eat insects, as well as centipedes, which eat insects and spiders. Sharks, which eat fish, dolphins, and seals, and frogs, which eat insects, are both examples of vertebrate carnivores.

Lions eat zebras and antelopes. They are vertebrate carnivores.

Racoons eat nuts, berries, and fish. They are vertebrate omnivores.

OMNIVORES

Omnivores feed on both plants and animals. Humans are omnivores. A crab is an example of an invertebrate omnivore. It eats worms, prawns, and seaweed. Bears eat berries and fish; squirrels eat nuts and birds' eggs. They are examples of vertebrate omnivores.

FOOD CHAINS

We have seen that animals can be put into groups according to what they eat. Scientists have studied what animals eat in their habitats and have linked the animals by the food that they eat. The links are joined together to make a food chain. A food chain shows how energy passes from one living thing to another in a habitat.

LINKS IN A FOOD CHAIN

A plant takes in the sunlight that falls on its leaves, carbon dioxide from the air, and water and minerals from the soil. It uses them to make nutrients. A plant is the first link in a food chain.

When herbivores and omnivores feed on a plant, they take in its nutrients, becoming the second link in the food chain. The third link is a carnivore or omnivore, which eats the herbivore or plant-eating omnivore, completing the food chain.

PREY AND PREDATORS

Animals that are eaten by other animals are called **prey**. Animals that eat other animals are called **predators**. In the three-link food chain on page 26, the rabbit is the prey and the fox is the predator. A food chain can have more than three links, like the one bellow.

This food chain has five links. The plant is eaten by the slug. The slug is prey for the frog. The frog is prey for the snake. The snake is prey for the heron.

HUMANS IN FOOD CHAINS

Humans are in food chains too. When a human eats a plant, they are the second link in the food chain.

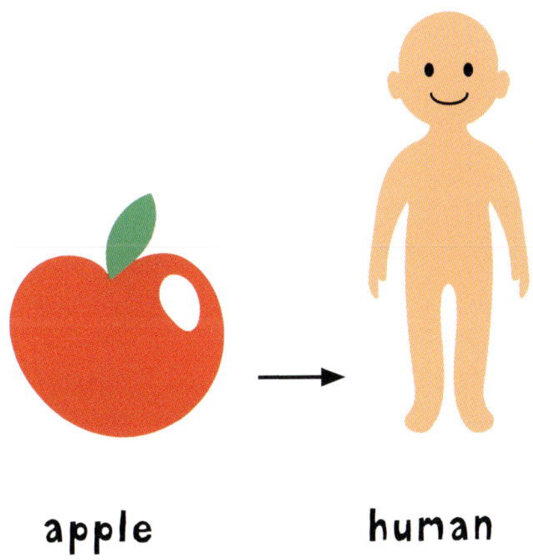

If a human eats meat, they become the third link in the food chain.

GLOSSARY

Absorb to take in. A sponge absorbs water. The small intestine absorbs nutrients.

Amphibian an animal that spends its early life in water and its later life as a land animal, such as a frog or toad.

Artery a tube in the circulatory system that takes blood away from the heart.

Bile a liquid that breaks up fats to aid digestion.

Brain the part of the body that controls all of the body's activities.

Carbohydrates nutrients that provide the body with energy in the form of sugars.

Carnivore an animal that eats other animals.

Cartilage the slippery and smooth covering of bones in a joint.

Contract to get shorter or smaller.

Digestive juice a liquid that breaks down food so it can dissolve in the water in the digestive system.

Exoskeleton a hard covering used to support and protect some invertebrates.

Fats a nutrient that provide the body with energy. Fat also creates a layer beneath the skin, which helps keep the body warm and protect some organs.

Fiber a material found in food made from plants that is not digested, but instead helps food move along the digestive system.

Food chain a group of living things linked together to show how they are related to each other by feeding. Food chains show how food and energy move from one living thing to another.

Germ a very tiny living thing that causes diseases and makes the body ill.

Gland a part of the body that makes chemicals for use in the body.

Habitat the usual home of a living thing.

Herbivore an animal that eats plants.

Ligament a cord that joins the bones together in a joint.

Mammal a vertebrate animal with fur or hair, such as a mouse, human, or bear. Most give birth to live babies that feed on milk from their mother.

Minerals a group of nutrients that are needed to build body parts.

MRI scanner a machine that uses a magnetic force to take pictures of what is inside the body.

Nerve a art of the body that carries messages from the sense organs to the brain and messages from the brain to other parts of the body.

Nutrient a material that is needed by the body for growth, injury repair, health, and all activities in the body that keep it alive.

Omnivore an animal that eats both plants and animals.

Oxygen a gas in the air that animals need to take in to survive.

Predator an animal that feeds on other animals.

Prey an animal that is eaten by other animals.

Proteins nutrients that provide materials to help the body grow and repair itself.

Reptile an animal, such as a crocodile, that has scaly skin and lays eggs on land.

Segment a section or part of something.

Sense one of the body's five ways of finding out about the world around it. Sight, smell, hearing, taste, and touch are our senses.

Spinal cord a long bundle of nerves that runs down the back inside the backbone.

Tendon a cord that attaches a muscle to a bone.

Thorax the chest of a vertebrate animal and the middle part of the body of an insect.

Torso the part of the body to which the head, arms, and legs are attached.

Vein a tube in the circulatory system that takes blood to the heart.

Vertebra one of the bones that make up the backbone.

Vitamin a nutrient found in foods such as fruits and vegetables. Vitamins help keep the body healthy.

X-ray an invisible light that can pass through the body. It can be used to make a photograph to show the position of bones.

ANSWERS TO THE ACTIVITIES AND QUESTIONS

Page 9: Muscles

Answer: Your biceps muscle gets softer and increases in length when your arm is straightened. Your triceps muscle gets harder and decreases in length when your arm is straightened.

Page 15: Teeth

Activity: The map will depend on how many teeth you have lost from your first set. Leave a gap in the map where a tooth is missing. You may want to make a map again, perhaps in a few months, and record any changes.

Page 23: A Balanced Diet

Activity: Examples you could include are red tomatoes, yellow bananas, blueberries, oranges, green peppers, and purple grapes.

FURTHER INFORMATION

BOOKS TO READ

Body Bits: Astounding Animal Body Facts by Paul Mason, Wayland

The Bright and Bold Human Body by Izzi Howell, Wayland

A Question of Science: Why Don't Your Eyeballs Fall Out? by Anna Claybourne, Wayland

WEBSITES

Take a closer look inside the human body!
35058.stem.org.uk/humanbody/index.html

Learn weird but true facts about the body with help from *National Geographic.*
kids.nationalgeographic.com/weird-but-true/article/humanbody2

Visit KidsHealth to learn all about how the human body works.
kidshealth.org/en/kids/center/htbw-main-page.html

NOTE TO PARENTS AND TEACHERS:

Every effort has been made by the publisher to ensure that these websites contain no inappropriate or offensive material. However, because of the nature of the internet, it is impossible to guarantee that the content of these sites will not be altered. We strongly advise that internet access is supervised by a responsible adult.

INDEX